Disney · PIXAR
FINDING DORY

CINESTORY COMIC

JOE BOOKS LTD

Published in the United States and Canada by Joe Books, Ltd.
567 Queen St W, Toronto, ON M5V 2B6
www.joebooks.com

Library and Archives Canada Cataloguing in Publication information is available upon request.
ISBN 978-1-98803-247-4 (Joe Books US edition)
ISBN 978-1-77275-298-4 (Joe Books ebook edition)
ISBN 978-1-44345-080-5 (HarperCollins Canadian edition)
ISBN 978-1-78585-786-7 (Titan UK edition)

First Joe Books, Ltd. edition: June 2016

CINESTORY COMIC

ADAPTATION, DESIGN, LETTERING, LAYOUT AND EDITING:
For Readhead Books:
Alberto Garrido, Ernesto Lovera, Ester Salguero, Salvador Navarro,
Rocío Salguero, Eduardo Alpuente, Heidi Roux, Aaron Sparrow,
Heather Penner and Carolynn Prior.

2

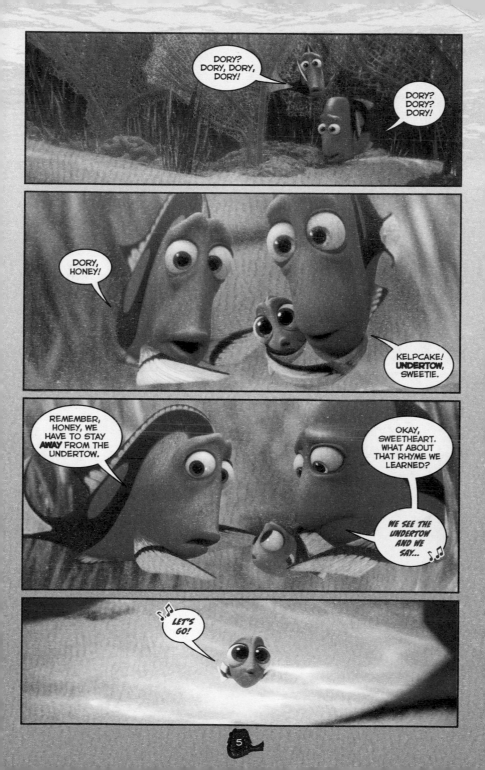

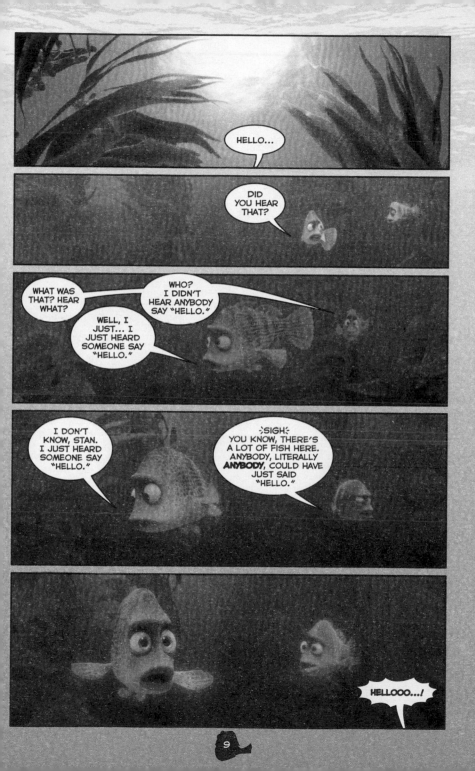

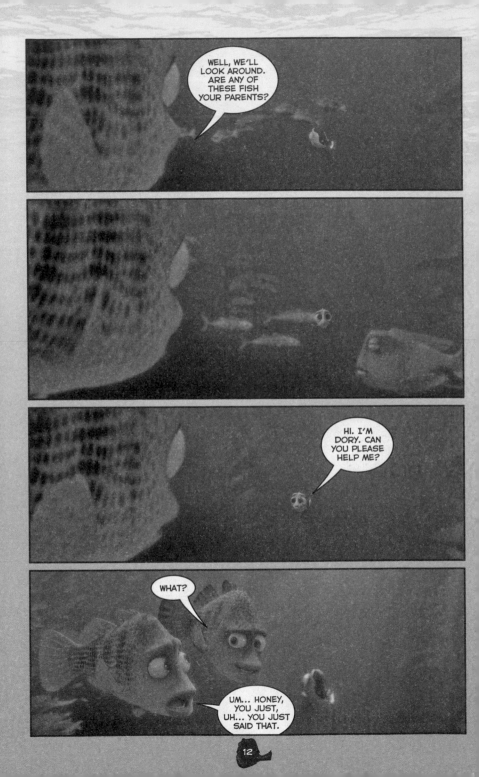

37

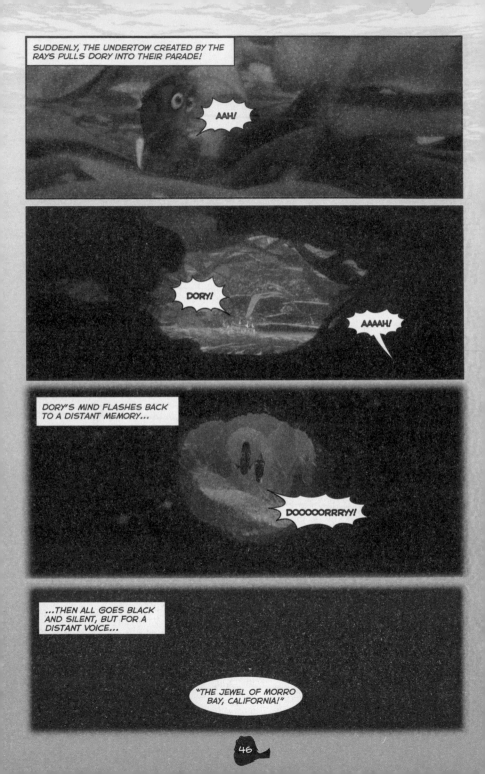

OH... I-I REMEMBERED SOMETHING... UH...

I REMEMBERED SOMETHING! I ACTUALLY REMEMBERED SOMETHING! SOMETHING IMPORTANT!

SOMETHING IMPORTANT? WHAT? WHAT WAS IT?

UGH... I'M NOT SURE ANYMORE... BUT I CAN STILL FEEL IT. IT'S... IT'S RIGHT THERE...

ALL RIGHT. THANK YOU, MR. RAY!

LATER, BACK AT SANDY PATCH SCHOOL...

OKAY, COME ON, COME ON, TRY TO REMEMBER BETTER... DON'T BE SUCH A **DORY**, DORY.

HMM. I DON'T KNOW. I-- HOLD ON. HOLD ON. OH. **OH!**

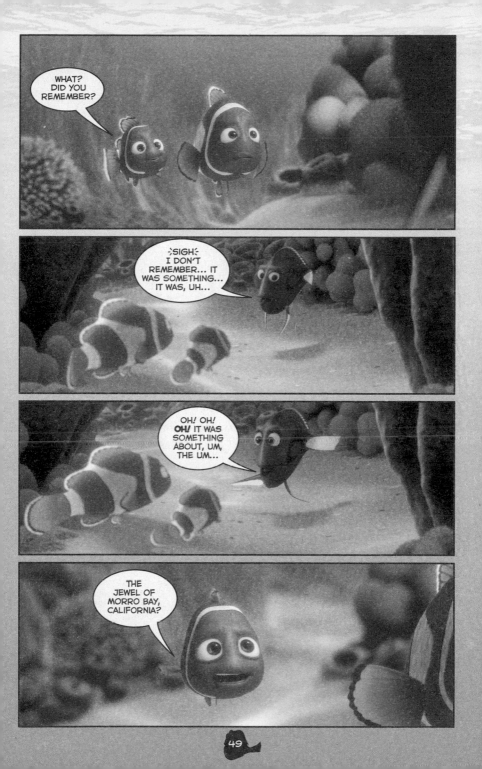

DORY REMEMBERS, IN A SUDDEN FLASH OF IMAGES...

GASP

58

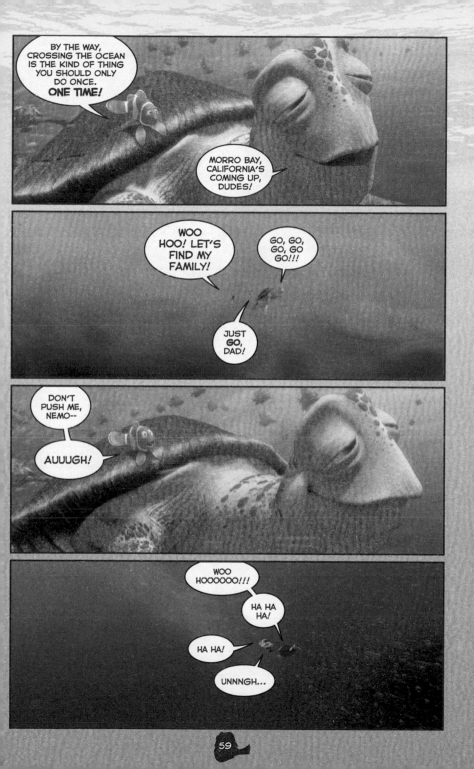

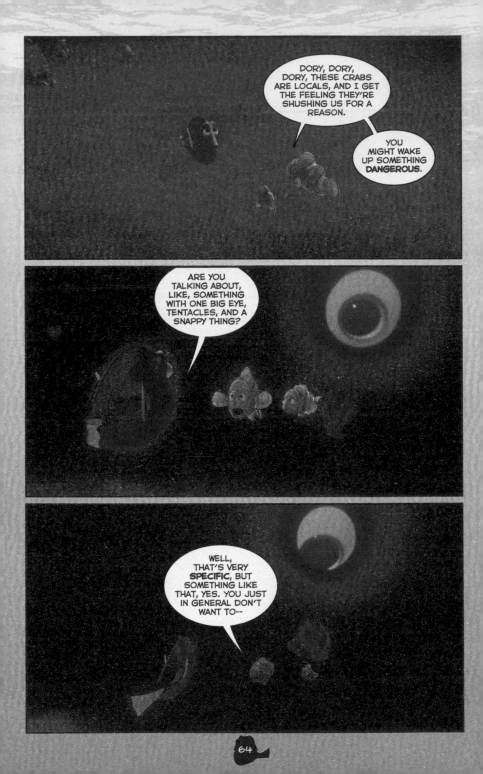

MARLIN, NEMO, AND DORY SWIM AWAY AS FAST AS THEIR FINS CAN CARRY THEM, PURSUED BY THE GIANT SQUID!

AAAH!

WHOOOAAAA! WHOA! SWIM FOR YOUR LIFE!

THE TRIO SWIMS THROUGH AN OLD SHIPPING CONTAINER...

...GETTING TANGLED IN A SIX-PACK RING, THE SQUID IN HOT PURSUIT!

AAAAARGH!

THOOM

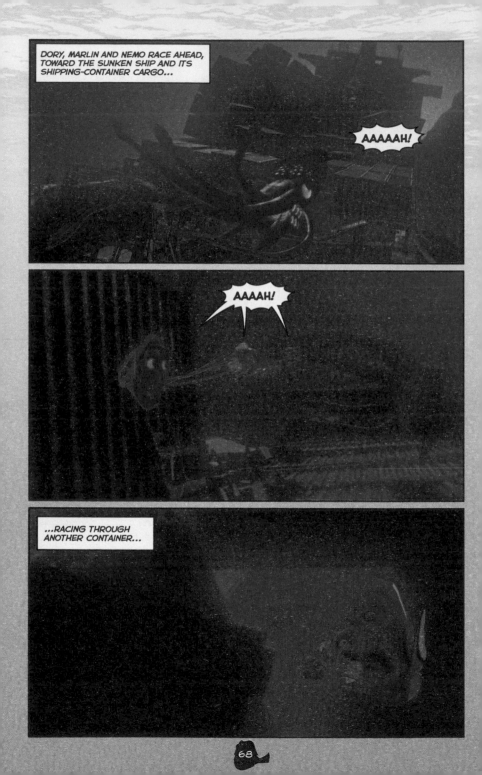

DORY, MARLIN AND NEMO RACE AHEAD, TOWARD THE SUNKEN SHIP AND ITS SHIPPING-CONTAINER CARGO...

AAAAAH!

AAAAH!

...RACING THROUGH ANOTHER CONTAINER...

...AND OUT THE OTHER SIDE, THROUGH AN OPENING TOO NARROW FOR THE PURSUING SQUID!

WAAAAUGH!

THE WEIGHT OF THE STRUGGLING SQUID IS TOO MUCH FOR THE PRECARIOUSLY BALANCED CONTAINER, AND IT BEGINS TO FALL...

...BUT ONE TENTACLE LASHES OUT...

...GRABBING NEMO!

AAH!

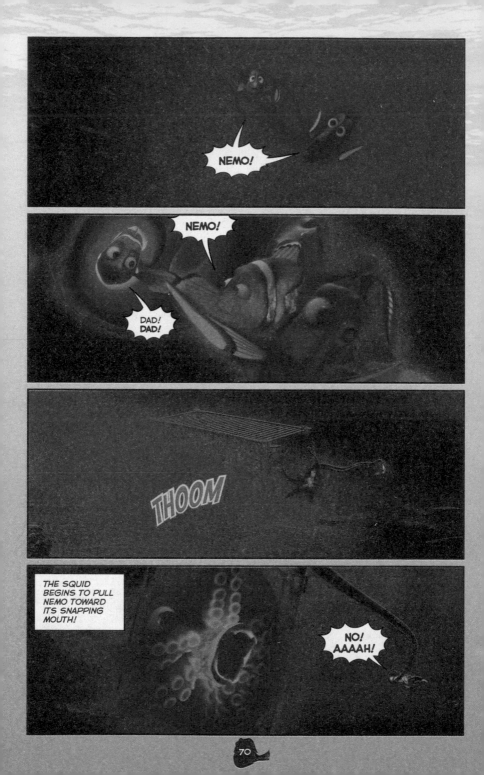

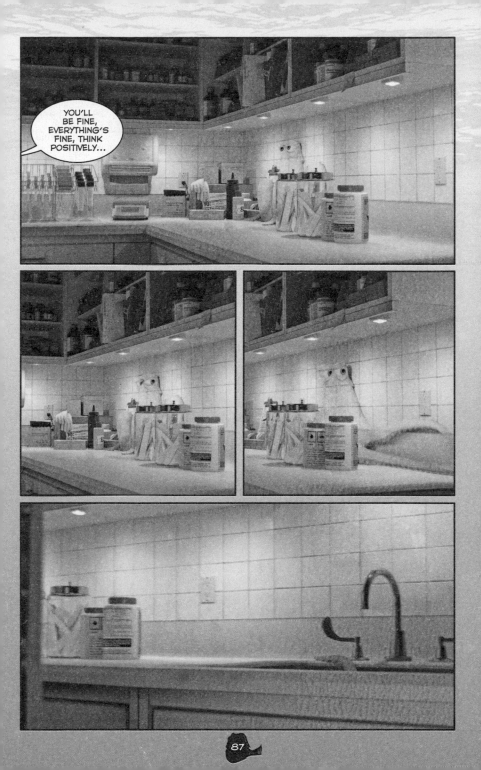

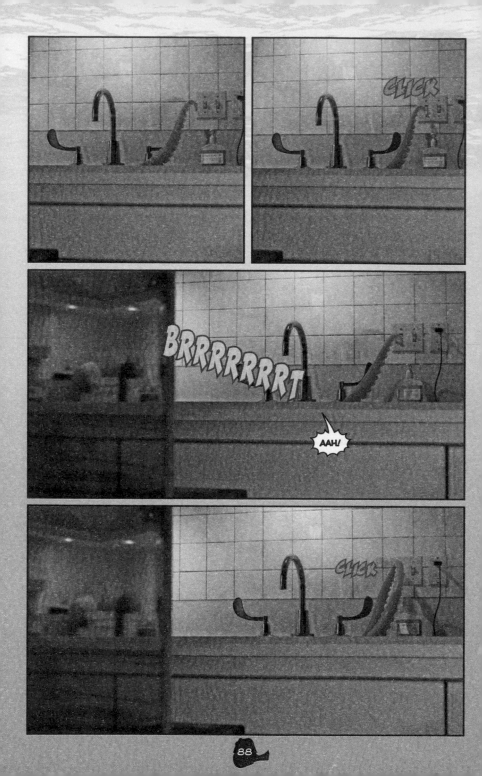

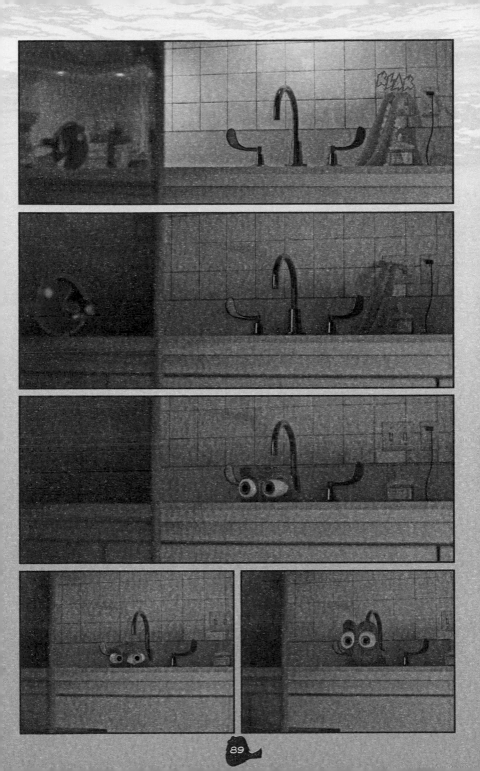

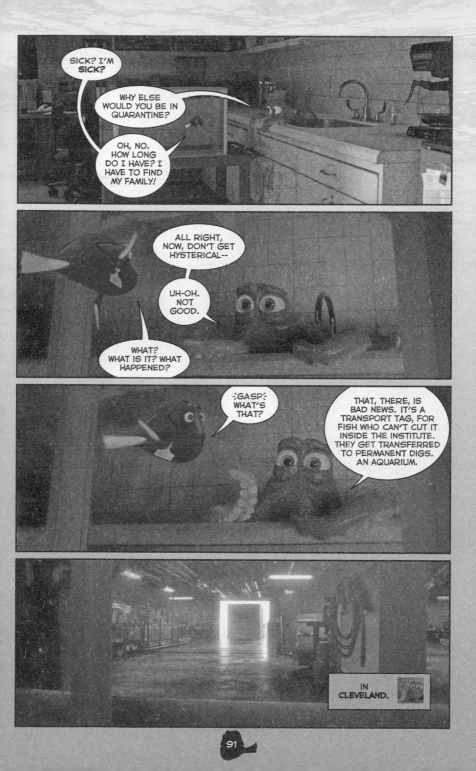

91

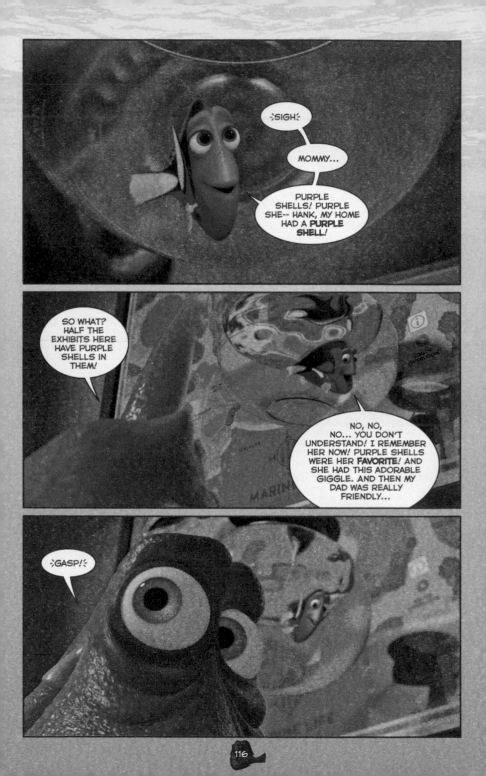

AND NOW YOUR WACKY MEMORY'S GONNA GET US CAUGHT.

HANK GOES DOWN THE HALL AND THROUGH A DOOR, BUT THE STAFFER IS HEADED THE SAME WAY!

117

120

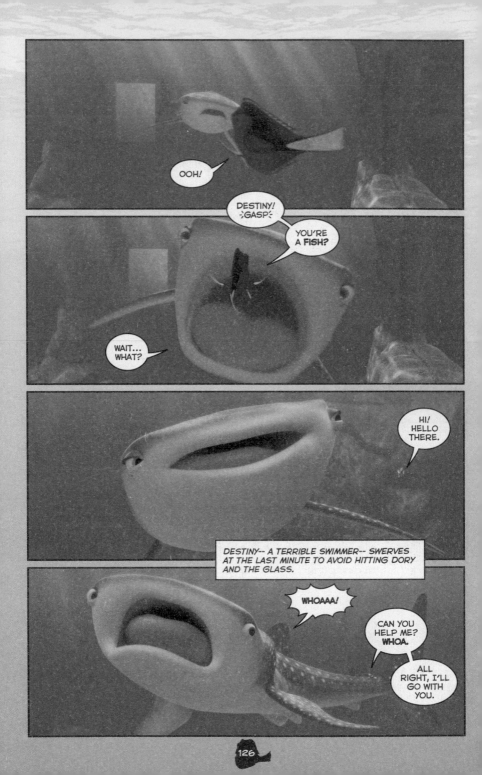

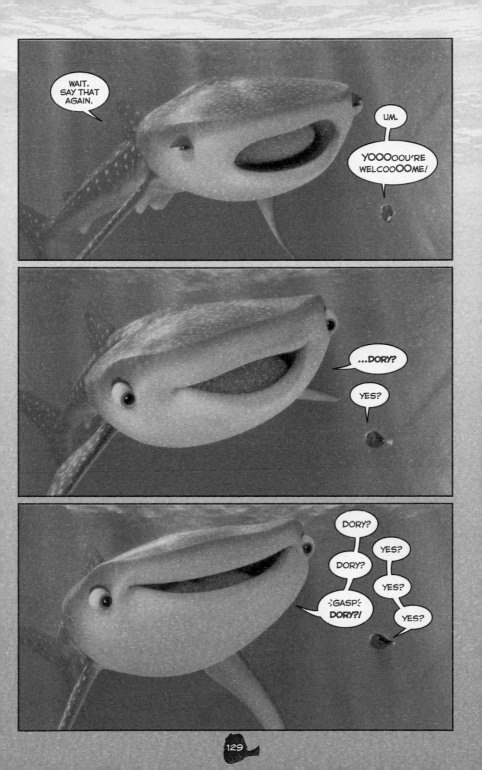

129

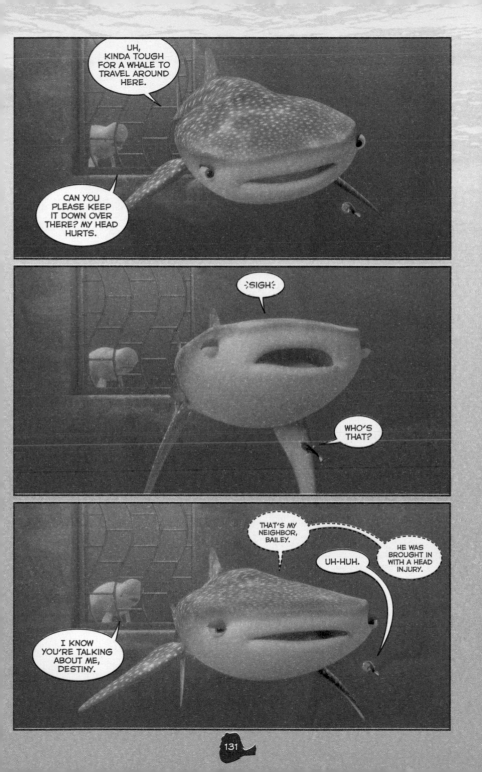

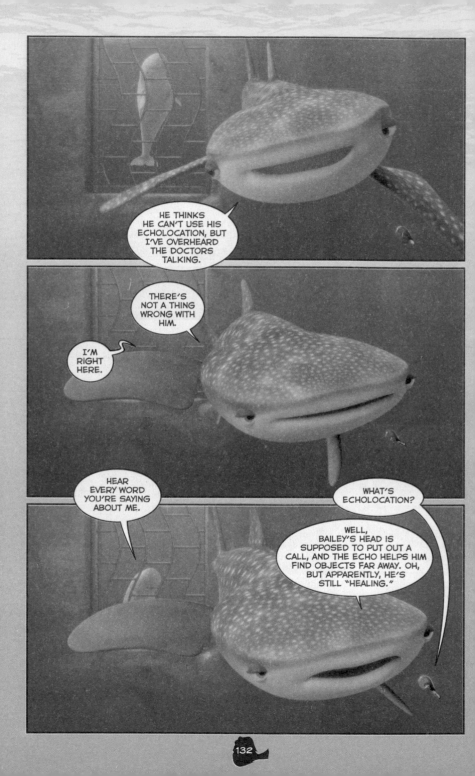

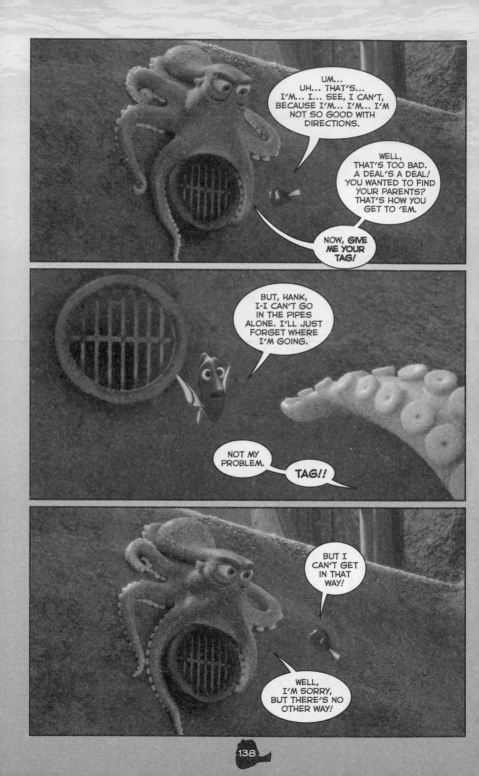

155

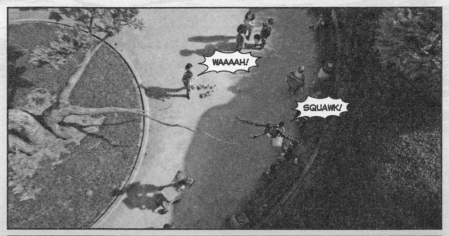

175

177

AS MARLIN YELLS TO BECKY, SOME OF THE WATER POURS OUT OF THE PAIL.

BECKY! BECKY?! LOO-LOO!—

SUDDENLY, THE BRANCH SNAPS BACK, SENDING NEMO AND MARLIN FLYING THROUGH THE AIR!

WAAAUGH!

AUUUGH!

THUP

THUMP

WHAT?

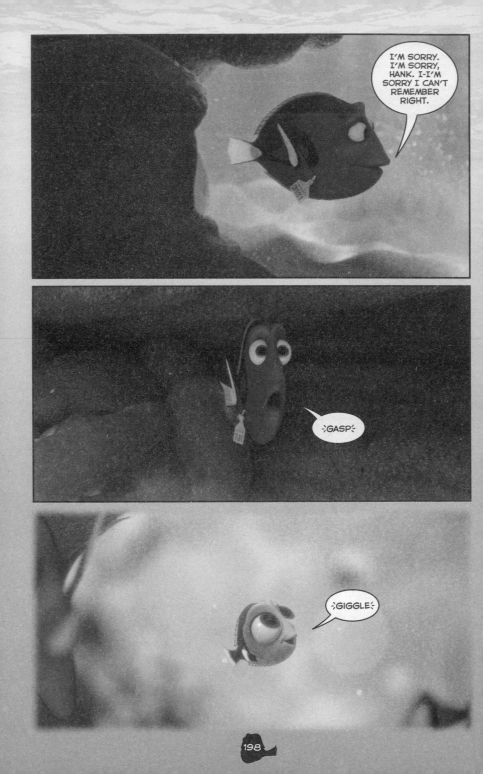

SPURRED ON BY THE MEMORY, DORY SWIMS FORWARD, FOLLOWING THE TRAIL OF SHELLS...

...MOM?
...DAD?

THEN, THROUGH AN OPENING IN THE GRASS, DORY SEES A PURPLE SHELL IN THE SAND.

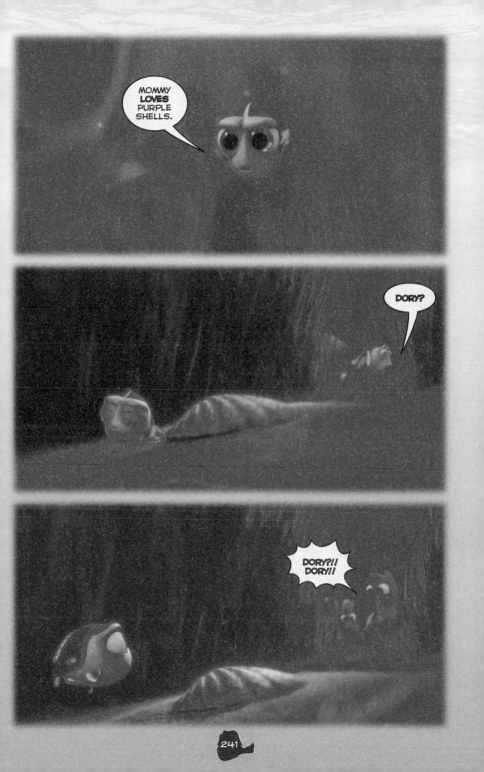

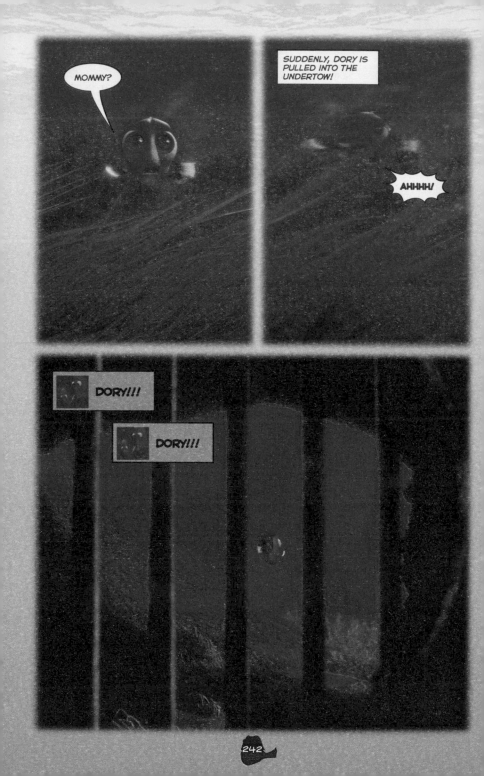

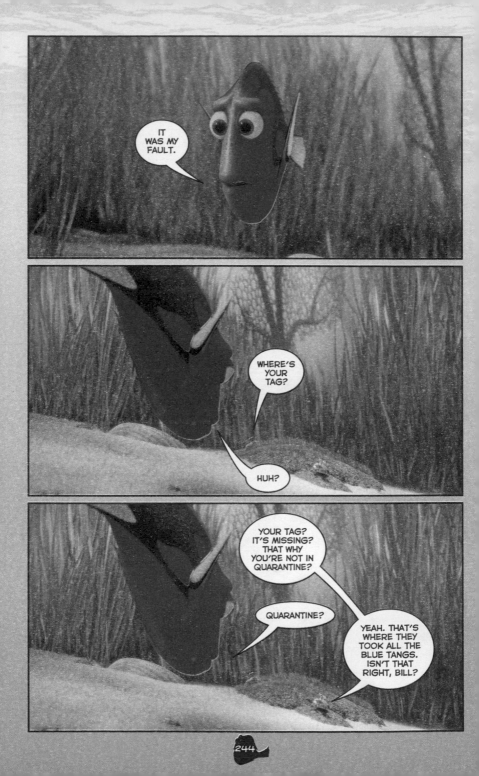

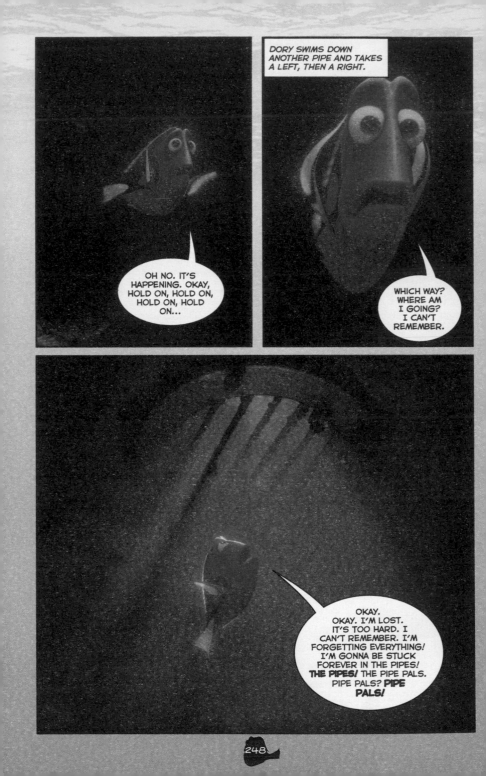

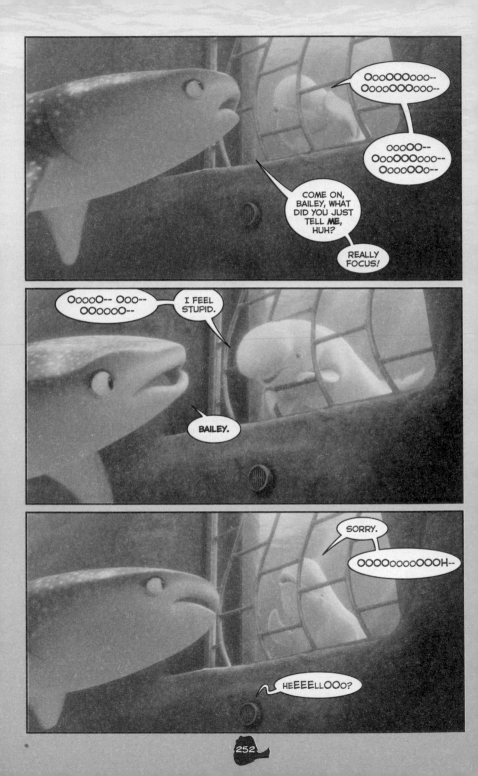

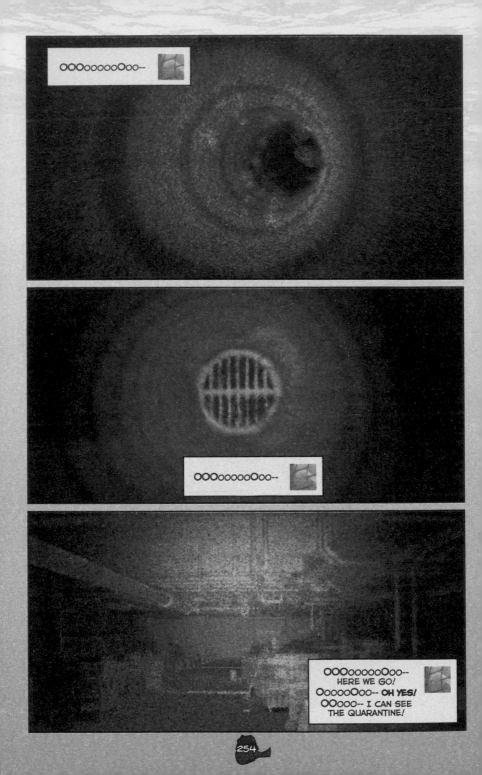

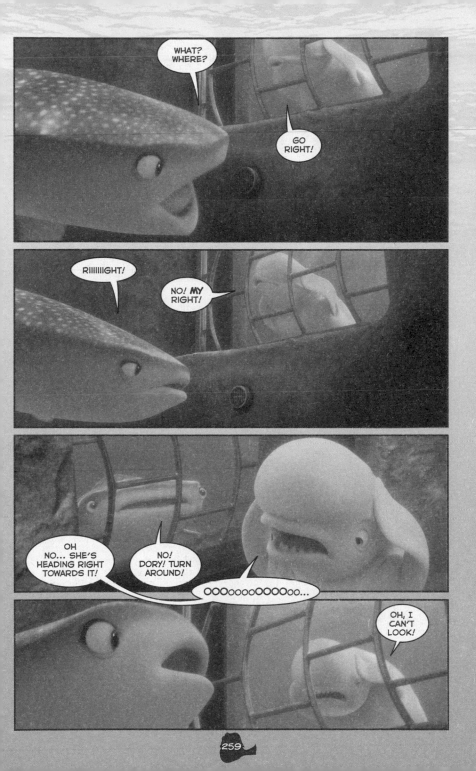

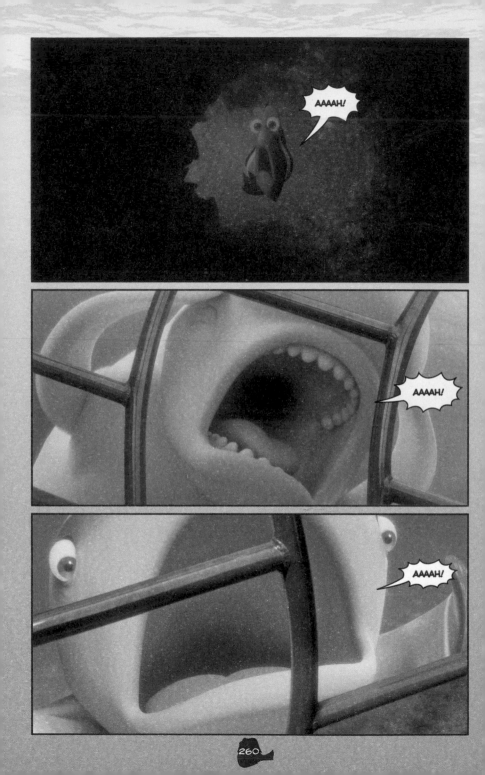

YOU'RE OKAY!

YOU FOUND ME! HOW DID YOU FIND ME?

THERE WAS A CRAZY CLAM! HE WOULDN'T STOP **TALKING!**

AND WE JUST **SLOWLY** BACKED AWAY FROM HIM AND INTO THESE PIPES. AND THEN WE JUST STARTED LOOKING.

DooOOOORY! I'M SooOOORRY!

OKAY, **WHAT** WAS THAT?!

HANG ON, I GOTTA TAKE THIS.

IT'S oooOOOKAY! SoOOORRY FOOOR WHAAAAT?!

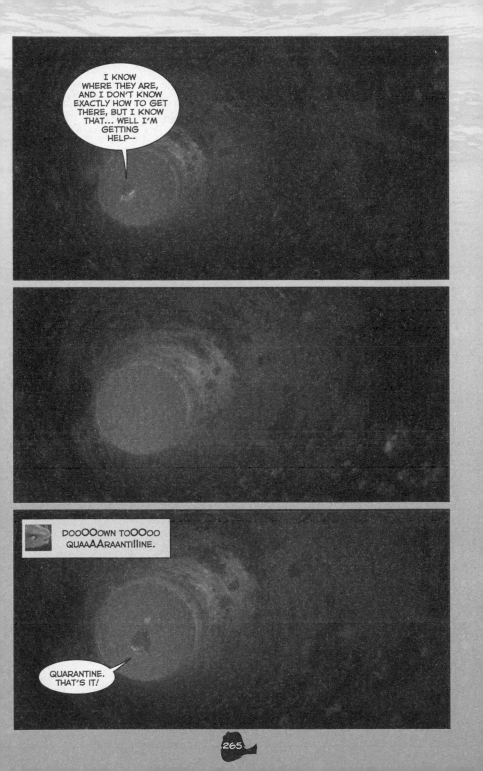

I KNOW WHERE THEY ARE, AND I DON'T KNOW EXACTLY HOW TO GET THERE, BUT I KNOW THAT... WELL I'M GETTING HELP--

DOoOOoWN toOOoo QUAaAAraantilIine.

QUARANTINE. THAT'S IT!

AS THE SUN SETS, TOURISTS EXIT THE PARK AND STAFFERS BEGIN THE PROCESS OF CLOSING THE INSTITUTE FOR THE NIGHT.

AT THE QUARANTINE LOADING DOCK, STAFFERS LINE UP TANKS TO LOAD ONTO A WAITING TRANSPORT TRUCK.

HEY, SO HOW MUCH MORE WE GOT LEFT TO LOAD?

UH, JUST THIS LAST ROW.

THE SOONER WE FINISH, THE SOONER THIS TRUCK GETS TO CLEVELAND.

WATCH THE TURN!

WATCH WHAT?

THUD

OW.

TOO LATE.

OKAY, I THINK WE'RE CLOSE.

DORY, MARLIN, AND NEMO FALL OUT OF THE PIPE AND INTO A TANK BELOW.

HI!

IS THIS QUARANTINE?

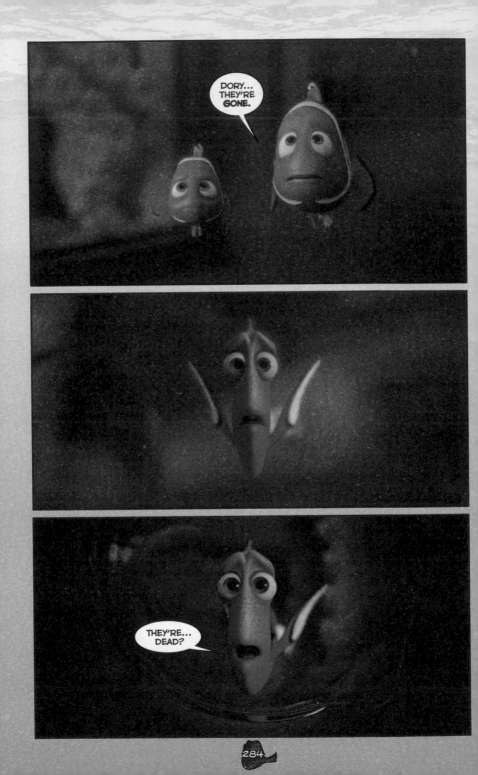

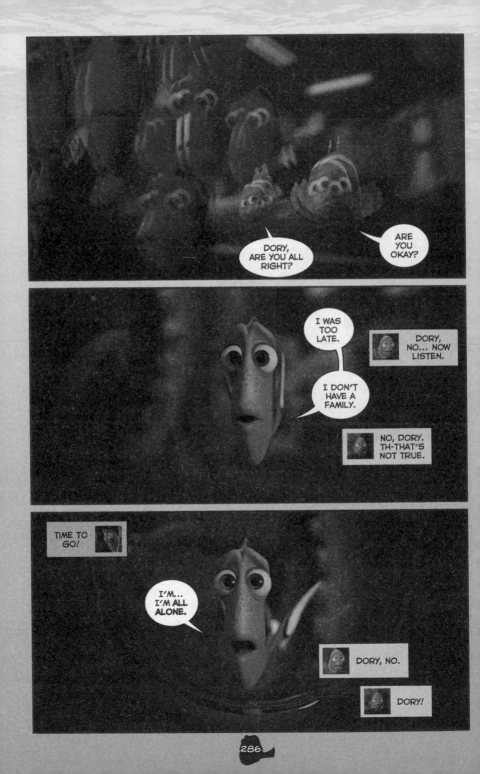

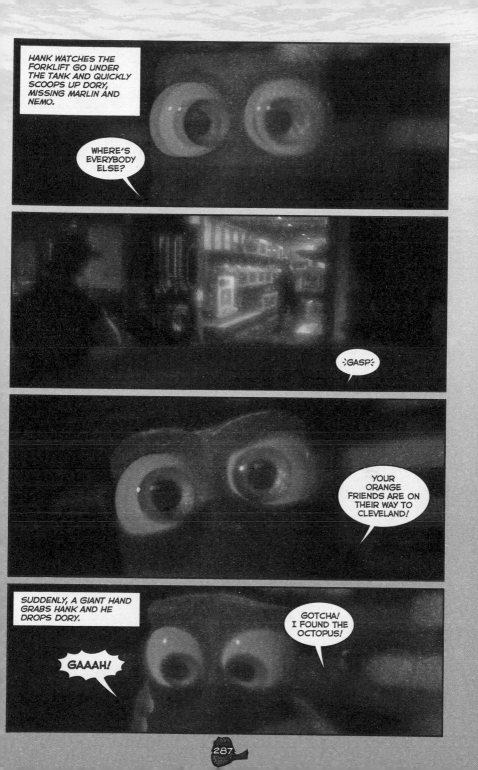

HANK WATCHES THE FORKLIFT GO UNDER THE TANK AND QUICKLY SCOOPS UP DORY, MISSING MARLIN AND NEMO.

WHERE'S EVERYBODY ELSE?

÷GASP÷

YOUR ORANGE FRIENDS ARE ON THEIR WAY TO CLEVELAND!

SUDDENLY, A GIANT HAND GRABS HANK AND HE DROPS DORY.

GOTCHA! I FOUND THE OCTOPUS!

GAAAH!

HANK SLAPS THE STAFFER AND SCURRIES TOWARD A NEARBY TANK TO CAMOUFLAGE.

AAH!

WHERE DID HE GO?

DORY SPILLS OUT ONTO THE FLOOR AND FALLS...

AHH! MOMMY! DADDY!

...INTO A DRAIN THAT LEADS TO THE OCEAN.

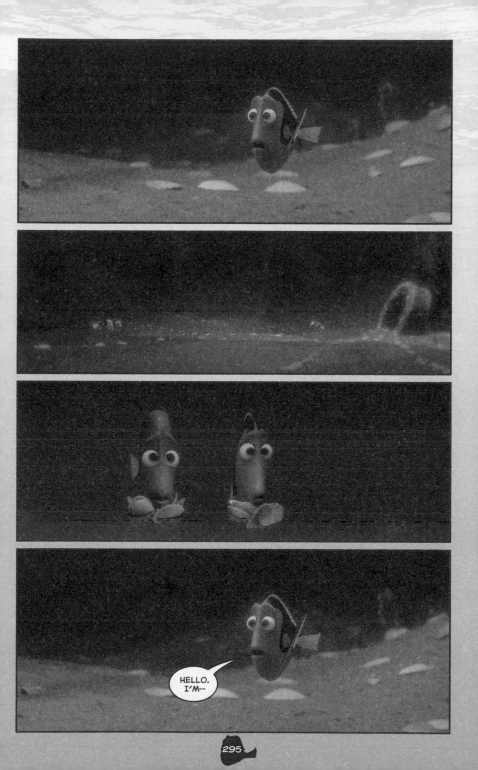

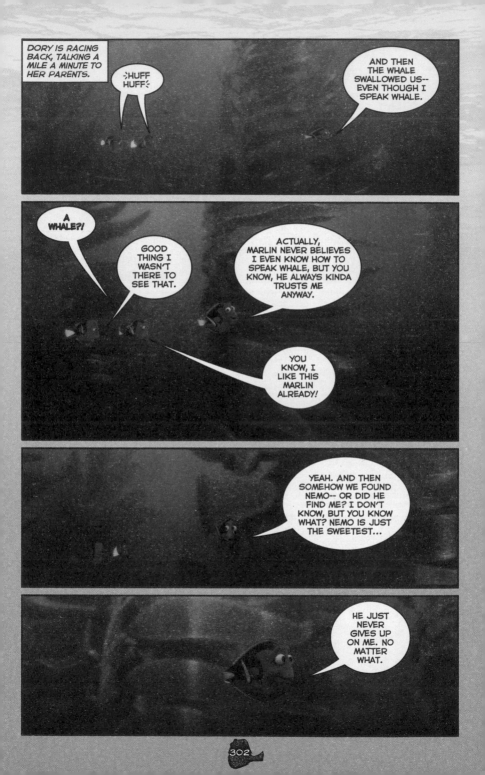

DORY IS RACING BACK, TALKING A MILE A MINUTE TO HER PARENTS.

:-HUFF HUFF-:

AND THEN THE WHALE SWALLOWED US-- EVEN THOUGH I SPEAK WHALE.

A WHALE?!

GOOD THING I WASN'T THERE TO SEE THAT.

ACTUALLY, MARLIN NEVER BELIEVES I EVEN KNOW HOW TO SPEAK WHALE, BUT YOU KNOW, HE ALWAYS KINDA TRUSTS ME ANYWAY.

YOU KNOW, I LIKE THIS MARLIN ALREADY!

YEAH. AND THEN SOMEHOW WE FOUND NEMO-- OR DID HE FIND ME? I DON'T KNOW, BUT YOU KNOW WHAT? NEMO IS JUST THE SWEETEST...

HE JUST NEVER GIVES UP ON ME. NO MATTER WHAT.

302

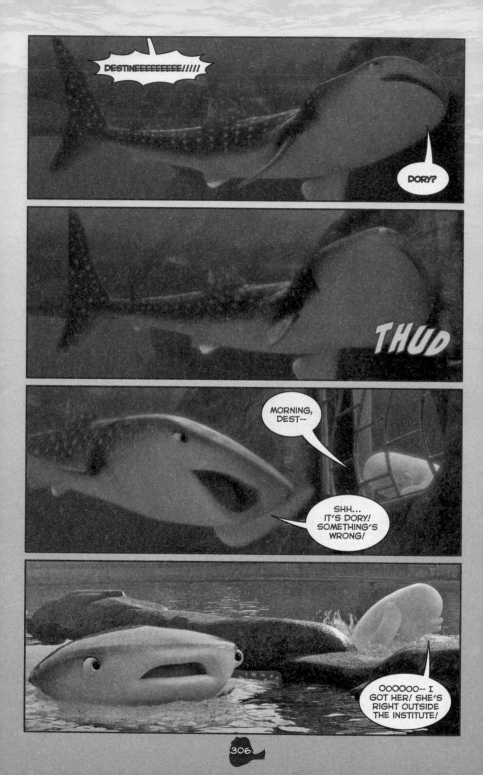

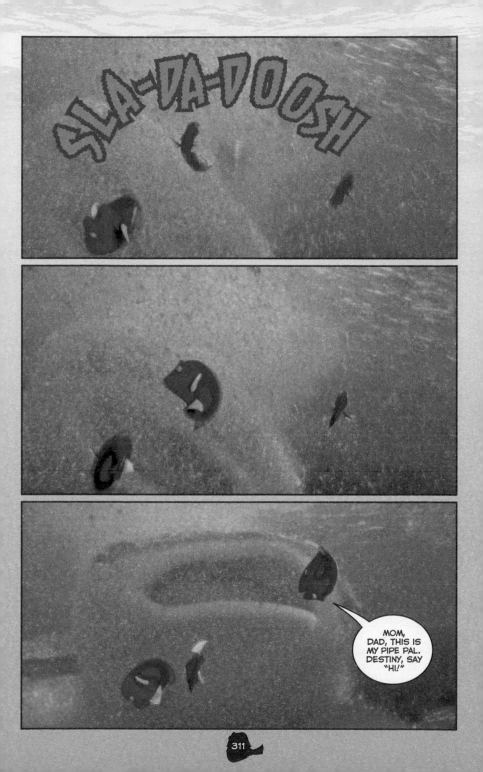

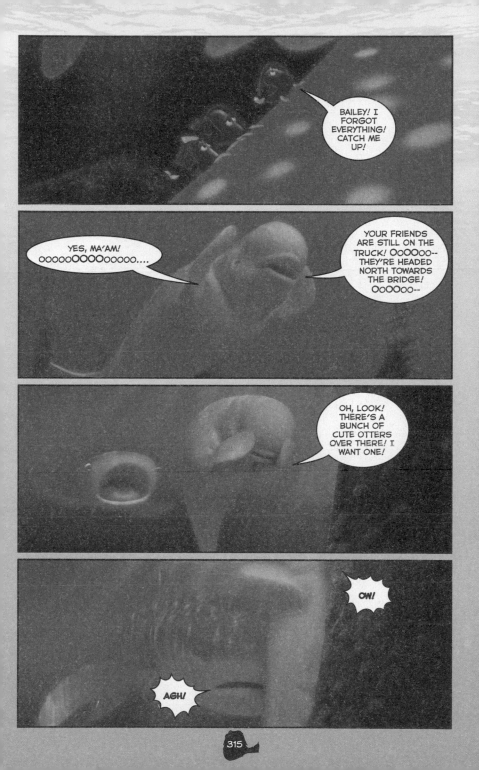

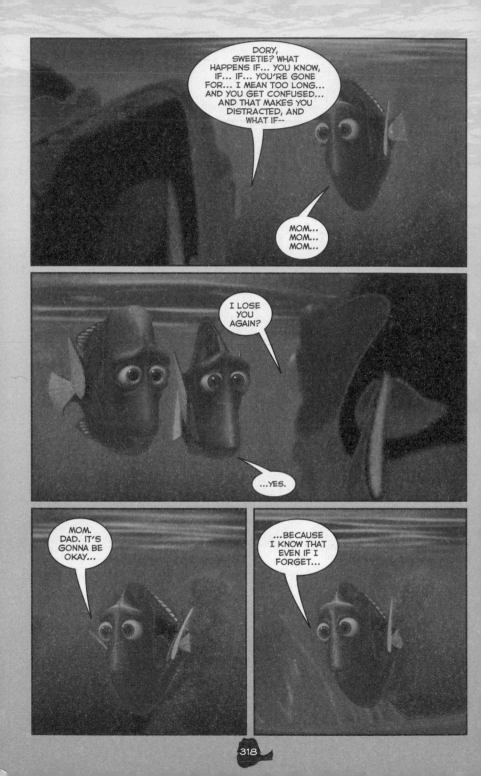

WELL, I DON'T **THINK** WE DID, AND THAT'S BECAUSE THE BEST THINGS HAPPEN BY CHANCE, BECAUSE THAT'S LIFE, AND THAT'S YOU BEING WITH ME, OUT IN THE OCEAN, NOT SAFE IN SOME STUPID GLASS BOX.

CAN I SAY SOMETHING?

I'M NOT DONE! A VOICE ONCE TOLD ME THAT ALL IT TAKES IS THREE SIMPLE STEPS: RESCUE, REHABILITATION, AND...

...UM... ONE OTHER THING THAT...

337

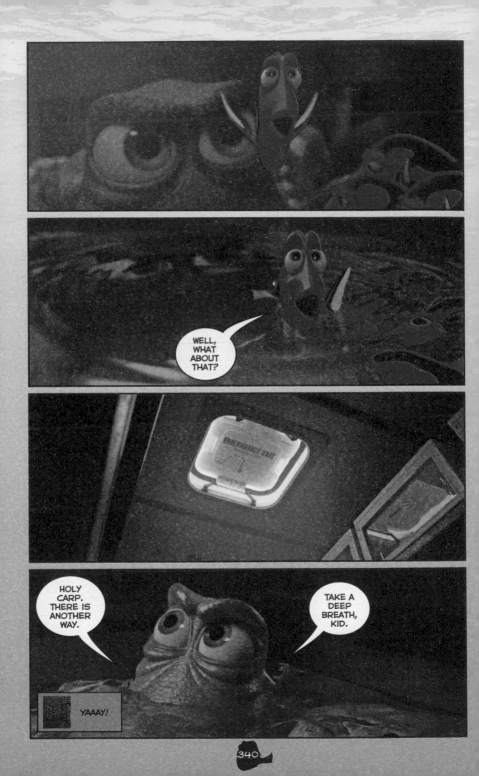

345

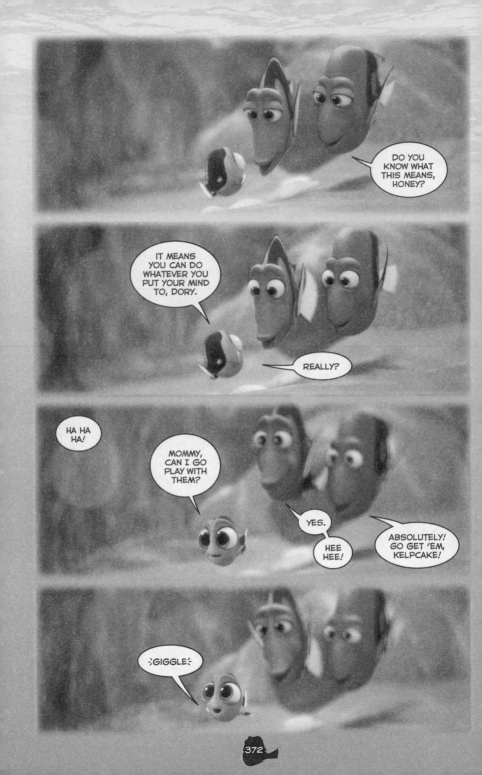

DIRECTOR
Andrew Stanton

CO-DIRECTOR
Angus MacLane

PRODUCER
Lindsey Collins

ORIGINAL STORY BY
Andrew Stanton

SCREENPLAY BY
Andrew Stanton
Victoria Strouse

ADDITIONAL SCREENPLAY MATERIAL BY
Bob Peterson

ADDITIONAL STORY MATERIAL BY
Angus MacLane